TRAVIS C. JENNINGS

LIFEGUARD

HELP IS ON THE WAY

ME
WE
MORE EXCELLENT
WAY ENTERPRISES

Publisher:
MEWE, LLC
Lithonia, GA
www.mewellc.com

First Edition
ISBN: 978-0-692-29917-3

For Worldwide Distribution
Printed in the USA

This book is dedicated to the memory of my grandmother, Ms. Fannie Mae Barber, who knew who I was destined to become and what I was destined to accomplish.

To my beautiful family: My wife and partner for life, Stephanie, whose constant love and consistent support knows no boundaries. I am honored to walk through this life with you. My children: Travis (my alpha), Briona, Da'ja, Desi and David Christopher (my omega), you are my world and I am humbled to be your Father. Daddy loves you all - infinitely.

To The Harvest Tabernacle Church family, a church like no other. I am so proud to be your Senior Pastor. We have matured in so many ways and you have pushed me past myself. You are the best. Destiny is calling and for us, the best is yet to come.

TRAVIS C. JENNINGS

LIFEGUARD

HELP IS ON THE WAY

ACKNOWLEDGEMENTS

The Bible says that without vision, the people perish. I also like to say that without people, there can be no vision. I stand in continued amazement at how God aligned circumstances, resources, support and the right group of people to strategically come together for the purpose of this prophetic movement that is - *the Lifeguard.*

When I initially ministered this life-changing message with one of my spiritual sons, I sincerely did not realize the immediate impact it would have on the lives of people who were literally "drowning" – but God knew. As the altar flooded with people even before the close of the message, then calls poured in after it aired on our weekly broadcast, the message of hope was now becoming a movement. Countless Facebook inboxes, Tweets, and more calls into our executive office continued to validate this God-inspired *Lifeguard* movement. I knew I needed a team of people who could envision this movement and accept any *Lifeguard* related task as an assignment.

This manuscript is a testimony of the grace, anointing, and power of God working in my life. I am continually honored by the fact that He chose me. I am deeply grateful for the inspiration and wisdom passed along to me from men and women both past and present. This list is long, but notably includes my spiritual covering, Apostle John Eckhardt – thank you.

I am grateful for my church family - the Pastors, Elders, Ministers, Prophets, Teachers, Deacons, and countless spiritual sons and daughters who believe in me and the great vision of the Harvest Tabernacle Church.

With regards to the direct production and development of this manuscript, I am very grateful for:

The support and patience of my wife, Pastor Stephanie L. Jennings – who knows she did not marry a man, but she married a vision and a mandate; my children who understand their father has a mandate from God. For this, I am eternally grateful for you. I love you all.

My personal "executor" for Prophet's House Publishing who tirelessly continues to stay on her assignment and coordinate all PHP matters and processes, Minister April Reason. Thank you.

Minister C. Dudley of MEWE, LLC, your professionalism, order, and excellence is second to none. Your dedication and commitment to completing this assignment is unparalleled. You are simply the best. Thank you.

FOREWORD

In Lifeguard, Travis Jennings gives prophetic insight to the plans of God for your life that are often unseen to the natural eye, but can be seen by the prophetic eye. The plans of hell to abort your destiny are really a part of God's plan to show his power and deliverance on your behalf.

Sometimes we are confused by our circumstances, and can easily despair. God's word is abundant with examples of God's rescue that are a part of His plan for our promotion. This book gives hope and understanding to those who find themselves in places that seem difficult and contrary to the will of God.

This book is both prophetic and creative in teaching God's power and mercy in deliverance and rescue. Deliverance is the major theme of Scripture. I am amazed at how God inspires us to understand this great subject, and Travis Jennings adds to the great wealth of knowledge and understanding of God's ways in delivering and rescuing his people.

We can never underestimate God's mercy and desire to rescue. The Lifeguard is the natural example of a spiritual truth: that God is our ultimate protector and rescuer. He will not let us down in the waters and storms of life, but will intervene and rescue us.

A drowning man is desperate for rescue. The Lifeguard has the responsibility and ability to save lives. Salvation is our inheritance. Deliverance and rescue is our portion. Let this book bring hope and faith on this truth. Let it minister to you as you read it. Meditate upon the principles that are taught.

I recommend this book because of its revelation and creative style, and because I know the author's desire to see God's people free and walking in destiny. This message is more than a sermon preached in a local church, but now a book that will touch countless lives around the world.

- John Eckhardt
Apostle, Teacher & Author

PREFACE

As a young boy growing up on the east side of Atlanta, my cousins and I looked forward to hanging out at the neighborhood pool each summer. Atlanta summers were hot, but the coolness of the water against my skin as I dove in somehow made the scorching sun just a backdrop to all of our summer fun.

Little did I know my love for the water, the beach, and swimming pools would one day yield a profound revelation that would become a message of hope to the world.

Fast forward. The year is 2014. My beautiful family and I are enjoying our annual summer vacation on the beach. My children's love for the water is apparent as they spend hours upon hours in the water. My wife is lounging beachside. A man sitting at the top of a 12-foot chair with a whistle around his neck and sunglasses on his face oddly catches my attention on this day. The lifeguard on his chair is a picture I often remember from when I was a child. This time, however, it was different. God invaded my vacation and began to download a prophetic, intrusive revelation about the purpose of the lifeguard.

This is the season for God's people to come out of any "drowning" predicament in which they may find themselves. Someone may be drowning in his finances, and here comes the Lifeguard. Someone may be sinking in the stress and the worry of life, but here comes the Lifeguard. Others may be overwhelmed by sin and distress--make way for the Lifeguard! The Lifeguard is here to save you, to float you back to dry land, and even to resuscitate you--so you can begin again, live again, and hope again. When life hurts and dreams fade, you can hope again!

It is the lifeguard's duty to watch and to keep order at the water. He remains on post with his ears and eyes sensitive to the faintest cry for help. Many believe that their situation may be too far gone or out of control, like they have drifted too far away from the shores of the beach and too far out of the reach of the lifeguard. But today I am here to declare that it is not God's will that anyone should drown in his or her poverty.

It is not God's will that anyone should drown in his perversion. It is not God's will that anyone should drown in her pain or even his pessimism. The divine Lifeguard comes to give you life today and to give you life more abundantly.

Although the lifeguard is skilled at saving lives, he must receive total cooperation and trust on the victim's part in order to ensure a successful rescue process. What's standing in the way of your full cooperation? What's standing in the way of your total trust?

I have come to give an announcement. This is the season that you're going to allow help to help. Now that help is here, this is the time for your divine rescue.

Although it may be hard for a water victim to cry out "help," the Lifeguard is alert and sees the struggle. Help is closer than you think.

CHAPTER 1

YOUR PLOT WAS GOD'S PLAN

When you find yourself in the midst of adversity and the enemy is telling you that you are a failure, put him under your feet by reminding him who you are according to the Word of God. You are a royal priesthood (see 1 Peter 2:9); you are the head and not the tail; you are above and not beneath (see Deuteronomy 28:13).

All things work together for your good (see Romans 8:28) and God will not leave you or forsake you when adversity comes (see Hebrews 13:5). Instead, God will watch over His Word to perform it in your life (see Jeremiah 1:12).

God wants the best for you. The Bible says, *"For I know the thoughts that I think toward you, saith the Lord, thoughts of peace, and not of evil, to give you an expected end"* (Jeremiah 29:11). God has a plan for your life.

David's life was filled with both adversity and triumph. From his life, we should be inspired to trust God and further understand that our plot was God's plan.

Prophet Samuel's Divine Assignment

David was the second and greatest king of Israel. He was also the youngest of his siblings and the eighth child of his father, Jesse, who came from the herdsman line of the family.

Although King Saul was on the throne at the time, God sent the Prophet Samuel on an assignment to anoint the next king of Israel (see 1 Samuel 16:1-3). While the people were still focused on the now, God had already moved to what was next.

The Prophet Samuel was on a divine assignment by God to anoint the next king. You may feel like you are a pauper. It may seem like you are in a defeated position. Realize this, it always takes a prophetic anointing to anoint the next thing. The word *anoint* actually means to smear.

In Bible times, when a priest or a prophet anointed an individual, it meant that he was launching that person into destiny. God has to smear us and prepare us for our next place in destiny. Not only are you intelligent, but God is also going to anoint you and give you the enabling power to get your assignment accomplished.

God is looking over religious people, and He's getting ready to anoint those who do not care more about secular things--dress codes, rules and regulations--than they do about being in the presence of God.

Also in Bible times, when a priest or a prophet would declare that someone was anointed to do a particular assignment, he had to smear that person with oil. The smeared oil represented the fact that the anointed person was now empowered to do what he or she had been called to do.

David Anointed as King

Samuel went to Bethlehem and entered the house of Jesse. Seven of Jesse's sons were in the house and all of them went before Samuel. He looked at them and said, "The Lord hath not chosen these" (1 Samuel 16:10). There was something missing in the seven sons who were in the house. It was a matter of the heart. The Bible says in 1 Samuel 16:7:

> *But the Lord said unto Samuel, Look not on his countenance, or on the height of his stature; because I have refused him: for the Lord seeth not as man seeth; for man looketh on the outward appearance, but the Lord looketh on the heart.*

Man looks upon the outward appearance, but God is looking for someone whose heart is perfect towards Him.

Jesse remembered that he had an eighth boy by the name of David, who was a shepherd working in the field. David came before Samuel and he anointed David to be king. God always raises up the forgotten ones.

David Defeats Goliath

King Saul was preparing the Israelites for battle against the Philistine army at the Valley of Elah (see 1 Samuel 17). Three of Jesse's oldest sons were on the battlefield, while David stayed in Bethlehem to tend to the sheep. David's life took an unexpected turn when his father sent him to the battlefield with some food for his brothers. David encountered a soldier by the name of Goliath, who stood tall like the sons on Anak (see Numbers 13:33). Goliath was about 9 feet and 6 inches tall and David stood only about 5 feet 2 inches tall. Let me help you to understand something. Little becomes much when you put it in the hands of God.

The Israelites, who were on the battlefield, were focused on David's age and his anatomy. Don't look at a person's anatomy; instead, look at the anointing, which is far greater. King Saul looked at David's anatomy and his age. Because of that, King Saul felt sorry for David and tried to give David his armor (see 1 Samuel 17:38-39). Saul was probably thinking: *You need to wear my armor because this guy is going to tear you apart.* David said to Saul, *"I cannot go with these; for I have not proved them. And David put them off him"* (1 Samuel 17:39). You cannot wear another man's armor when you yourself are in warfare. Your armor is tailor made just for you. You have to wear your own armor and trust that you are ready for battle with what God has given you.

David was confident that he would defeat the giant. He said, *"The Lord that delivered me out of the paw of the lion, and out of the paw of the bear, he will deliver me out of the hand of this Philistine"* (1 Samuel 17:37). God will always give you small tests as He prepares you for the final exam. Moreover, the enemy always tries to plot against the people of God, but your plot was God's plan.

4

You Will be Rescued from the Enemy

The enemy frequently thinks that he is going to destroy the people of God. Not only will the enemy plot against your faith and family, but he will also try to plot against your future. The Bible says that satan will get an advantage over us if we are ignorant of the devil's devices (see 2 Corinthians 2:11).

In addition, Luke 22:31 says, *"And the Lord said, Simon, Simon, behold, Satan hath desired to have you, that he may sift you as wheat"* and 1 Peter 5:8 says, *"Be sober, be vigilant; because your adversary the devil, as a roaring lion, walketh about, seeking whom he may devour."*

The devil plotted against Adam. Because Adam sinned, the enemy thought it was going to mess up God's creation. But God always raises up a Lifeguard. Anytime someone is drowning in their problems, perversions, or paralysis, God always raises up a Lifeguard!

God raised up a lifeguard by the name of Esther (see Esther 5). Jehosephat was surrounded by the enemy, but God raised up a prophet by the name of Jehaziel and told Jehosephat that this battle is not yours but it belongs to God (see 2 Chronicles 20:15).

The Plot against Joseph

In the story of Joseph, the Bible says, *"And when they saw him afar off, even before he came near unto them, they conspired against him to slay him. And they said one to another, Behold, this dreamer cometh"* (Genesis 37:18-19). Why would Joseph's own biological brothers try to plot

5

against him? The Bible explains that when they saw him from a distance, they said to each other, "Here comes that dreamer." Even though Joseph's brothers conspired to kill him, and eventually placed him in a pit, the plot was part of God's plan to move Joseph into his destiny.

God is getting ready to answer your life's questions. One of the questions you may have been asking is, "Why does the enemy hate me? Anytime I take two steps forward, the devil tries to knock me six steps backwards. Anytime I try to do what God wants me to do, that's when the devil comes in my mind and plays with my emotions." The devil hates dreamers, world changers, global shifters, movers and shakers, but God's plan always outweighs the plot of the enemy.

You might be dressed up and look really spiritual, but you may be drowning in a certain area of your life. Help is on the way! With each plot from the enemy, God always raises up a lifeguard.

What Is a Lifeguard?

A lifeguard is an expert swimmer who is employed to protect swimmers from drowning, accidents or other dangers. The key word is expert--someone who is skilled or is a master in something. Stop letting people who are not skilled try to help you. How can they help you if they have not been successful in the area in which you need the help? Romans 8:28 says, *"And we know that all things work together for good to them that love God, to them who are the called according to his purpose.*" I understand that the plot of the enemy serves a purpose. With no plot from the enemy, there's no plan from God.

The enemy's plot is only activated when you are walking in your purpose. Some of the stuff that we've been blaming the enemy for, I believe, is self-inflicted because the enemy does not need a plot if you are not working in purpose. If you are not working in purpose, you are not a threat.

Even if you are working in purpose, you don't have to worry because with each threat from the enemy, God always raises up a lifeguard.

Moses Becomes a Lifeguard

Moses finally said yes to the Lord's will for his life. When he and the children of Israel had almost crossed into their freedom, Moses was faced with a large body of water called the Red Sea. Right when it seemed like all was going to be lost, God told Moses to stretch out his hand (see Exodus 14:21) and the waters rose up to make a dry path for the children of Israel to cross over to the other shore. Amazingly, Moses stretched out his hand again, and the same waters that were parted for the children of Israel fell on the Egyptians as they were trying to cross over. This lets us know that where God is taking you, the enemy cannot go. Moses was a lifeguard.

Joshua's Journey as a Lifeguard

Joshua was also a lifeguard. He and the Israelites were on their way to the Promised Land, but they were stopped at the Jordan River (see Joshua 3). The enemy will always have a plot to discourage you right before you get to your promise. We serve a God who is bigger than what we go through. Don't give up because God has a plan. God has raised up lifeguards to save you from drowning.

When Joshua and the Israelites arrived at the Jordan River, it was flooded to capacity because it was harvest time. The Lord did not tell Joshua to stretch out a rod at the Jordan River like He told Moses. Instead, He told Joshua that *"as soon as the soles of the feet of the priests that bear the ark of the Lord, the Lord of all the earth, shall rest in the waters of Jordan, that the waters of Jordan shall be cut off from the waters that come down from above; and they shall stand upon an heap"* (Joshua 3:13). Even though the priests were entering a drowning situation, God was prepared and ready to assist them with the rescue.

God is also ready to rescue you. You don't have to live paycheck to paycheck. You don't always have to struggle. He is going to take the strain out of your struggle and He will strengthen you for this next stroke. He is going to raise up a lifeguard in your life.

Call for Help

When you are in a drowning situation, you have to learn to call for help. The enemy already knows that we can defeat him, but the question is, "When are you going to start believing it?" The redemption might hurt, but it starts with your cry for help.

8

Understand that lifeguards only jump in to save those who look to be in a vulnerable situation, not those who are playing around in the kiddy pool. The lifeguard will jump in to save those who look like they are at the end of their rope and it seems like they need some help. You have to just shout, *HELP!*

Some of you have been drowning or have been in a really bad situation and people have been offering help--but you said, "No, I'm good. Everything is okay." You have to stop acting like everything is all right. Don't wait until everything goes wrong to get help. Some of us could have avoided situations if we would have broken down our pride and said, "I need some help."

Have the Right Posture

I have even found out that lifeguards will jump in without hearing the voice of the person in trouble. After a devastating hurricane in 2005, helicopters were sent to save those who were drowning. I can imagine that the helicopters were so high up that pilots could not hear the voices of the people screaming. What they did see were the people needing help who had their hands lifted up. This is my posture when I'm going through trouble--I lift up my hands.

Even when it seems like God cannot hear you, I want to let you know that God sees you. God sees you and He wants to rescue you. If you are in a drowning predicament, you may need to change your posture. Do not keep your arms folded and lips sealed so no one knows you are drowning.

Today, you are going to give God the opposite of what the enemy expects you to give Him. Now is the time for you to change your posture. Instead of complaining, you can start consecration; instead of being pitiful, start praying; instead of being bitter, be forgiving. With every plot, God always has a plan.

You Are Next

If I'm sitting in a lifeguard chair, I cannot move until the replacement shows up, because I cannot take my eyes off the pool. There is a changing of the guard and you are next. God has anointed you to be a lifeguard. Pull your children out; pull your parents out! Stay in position. Your time is coming.

CHAPTER 2

SHARKS IN THE WATER

The first family was in heaven with God. Lucifer came against that family. The second family was composed of Adam and Eve in the Garden of Eden. The serpent came against that family. God's greatest creation is family, thus making family the devil's greatest threat. Since you are part of a family, the devil will place obstacles in your way to keep you from achieving prosperous and blessed family relationships. No matter what may be preventing you from being the person God wants you to be in your family, God is going to save and deliver you and your family.

God is going to raise up an intercessor in each and every one of our families, who will intercede and begin to war against the principalities and powers that fight against our families. We are going to have to stand in the gap and begin to pray.

Types of Relationships

God puts families together, and families are made up of relationships. Many people don't know how to deal with relationships. The temperaments and characteristics of others are hard to handle at times. We cannot judge and condemn someone just because of their choice of style or

11

color. Similarly, we cannot say that a person is going against God's Word because they do not like the things that we like. We must learn how to function in the midst of different personalities.

There is a difference between the types of relationships we have with the members of our families and the types of relationships we have with those we come in contact with on the everyday basis. As you read the descriptions below, try to determine where people in your family fit.

Thread – These are people we see on occasion but we have no emotional ties to them. There are plenty of thread type relationships at our jobs and at school. Perhaps, if this person was to pass away, God forbid, we might not cry, because we were not emotionally involved with them.

String – These are people we consider associates. We see them often but never really have meaningful conversations with them. The emotional ties may be thin, but they do exist. You may think that the thread and the string are the same, but they are different. They are different because if you put strings together, it will give you something beautiful. You can't really put thread together. Furthermore, a string relationship is a little weightier than the thread relationship.

Rope – These are people we see regularly and have conversations with, but the relationship lacks intimate details. This means we see each other, we talk, but we are not going to give them an intimate portion of who we are. We are only going to go so far.

Chord – These are people we see all the time and have conversations with intimate details, but we never share intimate details to the degree that shames us. For example, in a chord relationship you would say, "This happened to me. He did this to me. She did this to me. Can you believe they would do such a thing to me? " But you never tell what you did! You are always the hero. You are always the victim. You are never the perpetrator.

Cable – You will never go bungee jumping with a chord, rope, string, and definitely not a thread. The only tie strong enough for bungee jumping is a cable. A cable can last under any circumstances. We need cable relationships. We need people who will stay with us in the tough times. Some people you are trying to get out of your life are the very same people God put in your life; and some of the people you are trying to keep in your life are people that you must let go. Sometimes you are replacing a cable with a chord. One thing about a chord relationship--though you talk regularly, have intimate details, and they know your ins and outs, as soon as you get vulnerable and you are not the hero in the scenario, they are going to leave you. A cable relationship will be with you when all the chips are down.

All of these different types of relationships are now under attack. There are sharks in the water trying to devour the relationships that God gave you--relationships that are your kingdom connections.

Jesus Is Our Primary Lifeguard

As discussed in Chapter 1, a lifeguard is one who is responsible to ensure the safety of others from drowning. A lifeguard is vigilant, often sensing danger. A person who is drowning is responded to the moment the lifeguard senses trouble.

Jesus is vigilant, always watching, never sleeping or slumbering, always sensing and spotting any danger to our soul in our lives. Psalms 121:1-4 says, "*I will lift up mine eyes unto the hills, from whence cometh my help. My help cometh from the Lord, which made heaven and earth. He will not suffer thy foot to be moved: he that keepeth thee will not slumber. Behold, he that keepeth Israel shall neither slumber nor sleep.*" That means you have a lifeguard who watches over you even when you're not drowning. You do not serve a Lifeguard who takes shifts or takes naps. No, He is watching over you to save you in your drowning predicament. You may be flexing because you don't want people to know that you are on your last leg, but I guarantee, if you just throw your arms up and look towards heaven and say, "Help," the Lifeguard will show up and pull you out! He comes and rescues us!

The Lord does not want us to worry about anything; instead, He wants us to pray so that we will experience His peace. Tell Him what you need and thank Him for already manifesting whatever you need.

Attacks in the Family

Since we know that the devil hates God, we know that he will attempt to destroy anything that God loves. We know that God loves family. Examples of family are all throughout the Bible. The enemy will send spirits of discord that will attract sharks to make you believe that your family hates you and make you believe that nobody in your family understands you.

Understanding how the enemy operates is especially important for our young people. Have you compared your family with everyone else's family? Do you have friends who make you believe that your parents hate you? Do they try to convince you that your parents are always "tripping" and have so much against you? The enemy will have you linking up with people to escape from your family and have you becoming more loyal and connected to people whom God never called you to be connected with. You actually start crossing oceans for people who wouldn't jump a puddle for you.

Lifeguards are on post at beaches to warn swimmers of any dangers lurking in the waters by blowing their whistles. The enemy will send sharks to prey on your family, but we know that God has raised up lifeguards to help you out of your drowning, devastating, and disastrous situations.

The Plot of the Sharks

The plot of the sharks is to divide and conquer. This is nothing new. They did this back in ancient times. They divided the people and then they conquered. Below are three things that sharks cause in the family.

Division – Romans 16:17 says, *"I urge you brothers and sister to watch out for those who cause divisions and put obstacles in your way that are contrary to the teaching that you have learned. Keep away from them."* Schools of fish have to stay together because separately they are small. They

15

understand that if they stay together, they appear larger than they would if they swam alone. The enemy wants to keep you in your room instead of coming to the table for dinner. Deuteronomy: 32:30 says, *"One can chase a thousand but two can put ten thousand to flight."* If there are two parents in the house and two children in the house, the mother and father are standing together in prayer and faith believing God for more in their family and house. Two can put 10,000 to flight! The parents are putting 10,000 to flight. If you have two children in the house who are looking for trouble and not operating in the will of the Lord for their lives, you have 10,000 that are coming in. You have the mother and father putting 10,000 to flight and the son and the daughter letting 10,000 back in. So 10,000 from the mother and father minus 10,000 from the son and daughter equals zero; therefore, we experience a counteracting of a blessing--the household blessings have been counteracted.

Even though you are not in Egypt anymore, you are also not in the promise. Your family has been stuck in the wilderness. Because you are not moving backwards, you think everything is all right. No, it is not all right, because you are not moving forward either. You are operating in *just enough* when God has called us to *more than enough*. The blessings of the Lord have been counteracted so you are not moving forward nor moving backward; but God has sent lifeguards to bring balance back into your house so that you can move forward.

Discord – Proverbs 6:19 says, *"A false witness that speaketh lies soweth discord among brethren."* Discord is tension or strife resulting from lack of an agreement. The enemy will plant seeds of discord to divide your family. While the parents are praying for increase, the children are only trying to find the next "turn-on." In another instance, the children are trying to get themselves together and seek God while the parents are hiding their tithes and stealing their offerings.

The shark will try to run through the school of fish in order to cause confusion. We understand that a school of fish swims together so they can appear larger than what they would separately. When the sharks come in to divide and conquer, the schools of fish already know what to do. The family has to have a plan of action for when the enemy comes. 1 Corinthians 1:10 says, *"Agree with one another with what you say and that there be no division among you but that you be perfectly united in mind and thought."*

Everybody has to be united in mind and thought. You cannot expect people to understand what is not explained. Parents have to write the vision and make it plain (see Habakkuk 2:2). Be open and tell your children what the standard is in your household. Joshua 24:15 says, *"As for me and my house, we will serve the Lord."* It is a household thing. It is not good enough any longer for the parents to be saved and their children to go to hell. God will give you a lifeguard to keep you on course.

Differences – There is no perfect family. Jesus didn't have a perfect family. There will be some differences. Jesus was planted in a virgin girl's womb. (Luke 1:26-35) Scandal was raised as a result of His conception. Nobody in the whole world, since the beginning of time, had ever had a baby without having sex. So, Joseph was considered to be Jesus' stepfather. His aunts didn't even receive Him and accept Him until after he died. The list goes on and on but at the end of the day, everything came together and worked out.

Don't allow your differences to make you act differently. Attitude is a little thing that makes a big difference. The enemy will send in a listening ear, so that he can prey and play on the weaknesses of your family.

Ephesians 4:29 says, *"Let no corrupt talk come out of our mouth but only what is good for the building up that it may give grace to those who hear it."*

Be careful when sharing intimate details about your family in casual conversations and on social media. Everyone is not praying for you. Some are simply "preying." Some people don't have the grace to hear what you have to say about your family. You could be giving them the ammunition needed to go in for the kill. Give people building blocks and not bulldozers.

Saving Relationships

As a lifeguard, to save relationships, you must only give people the burden they can bear. I cannot give you a cable burden when you are a thread. It will break you. I cannot even give you a rope burden when you are a string. If you are in a pit, I can lower the rope and pull you out of the pit; but if you are in it and I lower a string, that string has little chance of holding you up. The integrity of the string won't be able to carry your weight. You don't need to connect with people who can't carry your weight.

Perhaps a teenage girl in her senior year of high school is praying to go to college and have great success, while all the other girls are going out all the time, drinking, smoking, and having sex. It would not be wise for her to be connected with such people who have no conviction. They say they love God, but they do not live holy. You have to start cutting people out of your life who cannot carry your weight. Your assignment is greater than your flesh. A chord is greater than a rope.

You will not find out some things until you're placed in a tragic experience and you will find out that a person is a chord instead of a cable. Sometimes the chords will wrap around your neck and try to choke the very life out of you.

We come to church and jump and shout, but we are still drowning. We have to wait on the Lord to rescue us and not rely on some temporary, artificial solution to our situation. Abraham waited twenty-five years. Jesus waited over three years. The earth has been waiting for Jesus for 2000 years. So when you put your situation in the scenario, keep on waiting on the Lord as it says in Psalm 27:14, *"Wait on the Lord: be of good courage, and he shall strengthen thine heart: wait, I say, on the Lord."*

Not only are we drowning but we are also bleeding. We are bleeding from division, from discord and from the differences of our families. We are bleeding in the water. Although a shark cannot see in the water, it has a keen sense of smell; and as soon as your blood hits the water, the shark is coming after you. God is getting ready to heal you of every wound, every cut, and every bruise that division, discord and differences have caused you.

Three Critical Areas to Protect

Sharks can smell blood as they are searching for wounded families. The shark was not even going in your direction, but you kept opening your mouth telling a cable problem to a string. The enemy will cause bleeding in the most critical areas in our lives: emotional, relational, and financial.

Emotional – Your soul is made up of your will, mind, and emotion. The reason why you think the way you do is because of rejection. Every person that's been divorced needs deliverance, because a spirit of rejection has come in and now the spirit of failure is on you. In your eyes, you think you will never make the mark and you cannot trust people because your soul is broken. You say, "I want to trust but can't. I want to love you but I can't, because if I buy into your vision, I will kill my vision." You don't even realize that your vision is this person's vision also. But your soul is broken. Who can bare a broken spirit? When your soul is broken, you are good for nothing. That's why you need a lifeguard to save you even with a broken soul.

Relational – When your soul is broken, your communication is broken. You have so much on the inside that you want to express, but it seems like you just cannot find the right words. You know what you want to say, but it never comes out. When it does come out, someone always gets hurt. Something always blows up. So we are also bleeding because we have broken communication.

Communication is a dialogue that someone has to release and another has to catch. We cannot catch at the same time and we cannot throw at the same time. You cannot assume and listen at the same time. Someone has to release. If communication is not received, you are talking at each other. We don't just have temperament problems, some of our problems are spiritual; and now a shark is in the water headed towards you because he smells that you are bleeding, and he's also coming at your family. Turn to the Lord during your trials; He is your lifeguard and the Lifeguard is here to save you from your drowning predicament.

Financial – You find yourself dealing with bad decisions regarding your finances. You are making unwise purchases. You have stretched yourself a bit too much. When a person is suffering financially, everything is ugly. Nothing looks good. The woman does not feel secure. The man is angry, and he feels inadequate because of bad financial decisions. You are bleeding and because of bad financial decisions, you don't trust each other anymore. When parents make bad decisions, children don't trust them anymore because they have not provided a stable household. Not being able to trust a parent can play on the psychology of a child.

My mother and father never raised me. I was raised in a roach and rat invested home. But amidst all the bad things that went on I received stability. I stayed there for eighteen years and within that eighteen years, we always had the same phone number. And then eighteen years before I came on the scene, that phone number was in existence. I have been gone know for about eighteen years and the phone number is still in existence. If I didn't get anything else, I learned stability.

We are bleeding emotionally, relationally, and financially. We are dealing with broken souls, broken emotions, bad decisions and we don't know how to communicate.

Did you need to go to college? Yes, but did you need to go to the college where the cost was so much more than you could afford? You were trying to keep up with an image and not education. Now you are working to pay off your college loans. You are struggling when you could have gone to the college that you could afford. You are bleeding. You come to church and everyone knows you are bleeding. One thing about a shark, he will come after you; he will come after blood.

Youth need to know that every time they are disrespectful to their parents, the shark smells it. Every time they are disobedient, he smells it. He waits for the perfect opportunity to get them by themselves to separate them from the pack. "They don't understand me. My mother doesn't understand me. I'm different." The devil has you so tricked. Guess what? Your mother said the same thing to her mother. That's the same spirit, it isn't new. That's an old spirit and it jumps on people who are broken.

We have some young people saying, "I'm the odd ball. I'm always in trouble." Some of them are "wanna-be thugs," but behind their masquerades, they are bleeding; they are drowning in their own blood.

Even in my emotional, relational, and financial bleeding, I am so glad that I serve a Savior who is a Lifeguard--here to rescue me out of any drowning predicament.

Some people think that their situation has to be big. The police do not have to come to the house and nobody has to be sent to the hospital to ask for help. It doesn't matter the amount of blood. The scrape on the knee that you neglected can get infected; and instead of curing it with some Neosporin and a Band-Aid, you have to get your leg amputated.

The shark doesn't need a great amount of blood, just a little bit. Your child heard you curse one time. You had someone coming to your house late at night. You say, "Don't worry about it." The Bible says, "*A little leaven leaveneth the whole lump*" (Galatians 5:9). In other words, a little sin will destroy a whole house.

A lifeguard never leaves home without a first aid kit. I don't care how large or small the cut is, there is a Band-Aid and there is some alcohol in the kit that can be used to heal you where you hurt.

When I was bleeding and hemorrhaging and sharks were coming from the north, south, east and west to devour me, Jesus came and rescued me. He is my Lifeguard. The enemy cannot destroy me.

You may have been bleeding and the sharks were coming after you and, all of a sudden, the Lifeguard showed up and saved your life. Every time the enemy comes after you say, "I have already been saved, so devil you can't have me."

From Victim to Victor

Know that Jesus is a Lifesaver. He saved your life. The Lifesaver is here. Tell yourself ...

I am not going to commit suicide.

I am not going into prostitution.

I am not smoking weed anymore.

I am not going to the club anymore.

When the shark of alcohol addiction calls you back, when the shark of smoking addiction calls you back, when the shark of depression calls you back, you can say with confidence, "The Lord delivered me from that. The Lifeguard set me free. I was in a drowning predicament, but now I am in a dynamic position to help save others."

I was looking at a YouTube video clip and it explained how the sharks will go after the surfers on their board. From the shark's view point, looking up from the bottom, the surfer looks like a seal. One of the surfers in the clip had a great testimony. He talked about how he was by himself in the water and a shark came and attacked his surfboard. He went on to say that a shark bit off one of his arms and one of his legs. He was so blessed to be alive and said he was still alive because he kept on fighting during the attack.

Sometimes in the midst of an attack, we just lie down and take it. No! You have to get to the point where you say, "I am not taking it any more. My family is not going through this anymore. I am fighting back. I will not die."

I dare parents to become their children's number one intercessors and confess: My child is not going out like this. My child will not give up. I am not giving up on my baby. Every prophecy that has been spoken over my life, over my household, over my family, I am fighting for it. I cannot quit. I will not quit.

You are victorious. *"And from the days of John the Baptist until now the kingdom of heaven suffereth violence, and the violent take it by force"* (Matthew 11:12). You have to keep fighting. You have seen too much; you have heard too much to lie down and do nothing. You know what the Lord can do. You have seen Him heal. You have seen Him deliver.

The same guy that got bitten by the shark saw help coming. When he saw help coming, his adrenaline kicked in and he began to fight the shark harder. Tell yourself, *Help is on the way!*

With boldness, tell the enemy, "I am not giving up. I am going to have a mind altering experience. I will let that mind be in me that was also in Christ Jesus." (see Philippians 2:5). My house and my children's houses and their children's houses will be blessed. The sharks of division, discord, and

25

differences cannot destroy the destiny on my life. I am taking my authority back. This is my life and I have authority to call those things that be not as though they were (see Romans 4:17). Therefore, I call into my life: healing and health, blessings and favor, goodness and mercy. I'm fighting for every prophecy, every promise, and every principle.

The fight just got real. I dare you to praise Him for your rescue. The Lifeguard is here!

CHAPTER 3

HE RESCUED ME FROM DROWNING

He rescued me from drowning! In these last and evil days, anytime God wants to do something, He will always raise up a lifeguard in the midst of it all to save His people from trouble and from danger. When the children of Israel faced the Red Sea, God raised up a lifeguard by the name of Moses. When they were facing the Jordan River, God raised up a lifeguard by the name of Joshua. The Bible also tells us that when Haman tried to destroy the Jews, God raised up a lifeguard by the name of Esther.

Any time the people of God are in danger, God will always raise up a lifeguard. When Moses encountered the Red Sea, he didn't call for an army; instead, he called on God. Similarly, when Joshua went against Jericho, he didn't call for bombs; he called on God. When the three Hebrew boys were facing the fiery furnace, they didn't call for a fireman; they too called on God. When Daniel was facing the lion's den, he did not call for animal control; he called on the One who is in control; he called on God. When Nehemiah saw the destruction of the city, he didn't call for a planning committee; he called on God for help--the One who has a plan for all of our lives.

Peter, by faith, walked on water and when he started sinking, he didn't call for a sailboat; he called on God for help. Help is on the way!

> *And straightway Jesus constrained his disciples to get into a ship, and to go before him unto the other side, while he sent the multitudes away. And when he had sent the multitudes away, he went up into a mountain apart to pray: and when the evening was come, he was there alone. But the ship was now in the midst of the sea, tossed with waves: for the wind was contrary. And in the fourth watch of the night Jesus went unto them, walking on the sea. And when the disciples saw him walking on the sea, they were troubled, saying, It is a spirit; and they cried out for fear. But straightway Jesus spake unto them, saying, Be of good cheer; it is I; be not afraid. And Peter answered him and said, Lord, if it be thou, bid me come unto thee on the water. And he said, Come. And when Peter was come down out of the ship, he walked on the water, to go to Jesus. But when he saw the wind boisterous, he was afraid; and beginning to sink, he cried, saying, Lord, save me. And immediately Jesus stretched forth his hand, and caught him, and said unto him, O thou of little faith, wherefore didst thou doubt?* (Matthew 14: 22-31)

I know you may be going through a drowning predicament; your back is up against the wall and it seems like you're not coming out. I am here to tell you that God is going to bring you all the way out. I don't care what it is or who it is or how long you've been stuck in it. God has the power to bring you all the way out. How do I know? Because God always raises up a lifeguard!

It is the job of the lifeguard to watch over God's people and to make sure that they are safe and secure. The lifeguard's job is not to only save you from drowning, but also to maintain order at the pool. The enemy has been trying to fight against you and destroy you and have your life in chaos, but the lifeguard is bringing order to your house!

It is the job of the lifeguard to make sure that he or she is properly trained in CPR. God knows how to bring you back from the dead! The lifeguard supervises swimmers, seeks out hazardous conditions and prevents incidents and accidents. The lifeguard also gives advice on water safety and controls unruly behavior. The job can be boring at times when the pool is quiet or it can be scary when the pool is very busy.

Lifeguards are highly trained in resuscitation and CPR. God spoke to me and said there are a lot of people, even in the church, who are drowning from the pressure, perversion, or some type of predicament. Whatever the problem is, God knows how to raise up a lifeguard to get you up out of your circumstance. When you cry out for help, help shows up! *"God is our refuge and strength, a very present help in trouble"* (Psalm 46:1). We have a

29

lifeguard and His name is Jesus. We have a lifeguard and His name is Emmanuel. We have a lifeguard and His name is Jireh! Not only is He strong and mighty but He is also mighty in the midst of your battle. God is sending help!

Peter's Lifeguard in the Storm

I want to revisit the story of Peter walking on water as told in chapter 14 of the book of Matthew, which is the longest of the synoptic gospels. There are three things that are discovered in this passage of Scripture:

1) Jesus' devotion

2) The disciples' dilemma

3) Peter's desperation

After the feeding of the five thousand, which did not include women and children, Jesus sends His disciples ahead of Him in a boat across the Sea of Galilee. Several hours later in the night, the disciples enter a storm during the fourth watch, which is between 3 a.m. and 6 a.m. Verse 23 says, *"And when he had sent the multitudes away, he went up into a mountain apart to pray: and when the evening was come, he was there alone."* Notice the Scripture says He was there alone. So, we see Jesus' devotion. We understand that before Jesus did any miracles, performances or declarations of power, there had to be a devotion of intimacy.

There is pureness, priority, and then the performance. He was pure in His heart towards the things of His Father. Even after feeding the 5,000 Jesus could have gotten lifted up in pride, but He drew himself away to a mountain to pray.

What do we do after we experience the greatest things of our lives? What do we do after experiencing great success? Do we draw away into prayer or do we stay in the limelight? Jesus drew away. He spent time with God, and Jesus is our example.

If you really want power, it only comes through prayer. He was drawn away into prayer! After Jesus' devotion, we see the disciples' dilemma. When the disciples saw Jesus walking on the sea, they were troubled. Verse 26 says, *"And when the disciples saw him walking on the sea, they were troubled, saying, It is a spirit; and they cried out for fear."*

So, Jesus heard His disciples' outcry after His devotion in the fourth watch. If you are an intercessor, you understand that the fourth watch is when the commanders of the morning, the prophetic people, begin to open up their mouths and seek the face of God. They begin to download from heaven what God wants to do in the earthly realm. They begin to prophecy in the fourth watch, which is again between 3 a.m. and 6 a.m.

It is the darkest hour but it is also the most productive hour. Jesus shows up in the darkest hour. I don't care how dark or gloomy your hour is, Jesus always shows up in the darkest of hours. He shows up in the lion's den. He shows up in the fiery furnace. The darkest hour is just before daybreak! If you are going through one of the darkest hours in your life, Jesus will show up and turn the darkness into light; and whatever is wrong, He will make it right. Even the high places, He brings down.

31

I cannot understand how people just come to church and have no relationship with Christ after they leave the four walls behind. Jesus, even after He had devotion, even after He came out of prayer, performed. He came out of the mountain; He walked on the mountain and went from the mountain to the sea. Jesus came out of prayer and then went on to perform.

Could it be that if there is no private prayer, there cannot be any public performance? What we've been seeing in the body of Christ is a whole lot of public performance and no private prayer. That's why you can sing and be a fornicator and you can preach and yet be a liar. There is no private prayer.

Jesus comes out of prayer and He walks on the mountain, then He walks in the sand, then He walks on the rocks. In between the rock, sand and mountains, He walks on water. Before Jesus came, the disciples had been struggling for at least nine to ten hours. They had been frantic for a long time. Jesus did not come at the start of the trouble, but He came at the end of the trouble. Because when He comes, the trouble has to cease. The raging tempest has to cease.

The struggle was over in the fourth watch--the time where little becomes much, where miracles are made manifest. We see Jesus' devotion. We see the disciples' deliverance.

Notice that the disciples never called for Jesus to come. Likewise, the three Hebrew boys needed deliverance; Moses, at the Red Sea, needed deliverance; and Joshua, at

Jericho, needed deliverance, but none of these men of God called for help. That's why in Isaiah 65:24, it says, *"And it shall come to pass, that before they call, I will answer; and while they are yet speaking, I will hear."* God is about to show up in your life and He's about to make the storm cease before you even open your mouth. God is going to answer some prayers before you even pray about them. Amen!

As I mentioned previously, not only is Jesus a Lifeguard, but we also become lifeguards in our families, on our jobs, and even in our communities. As lifeguards, it is important for us to understand that there are seven elements to rescuing someone. In order to have a successful rescue, the elements must be known, understood, and carried out.

1) **Identification** – The first thing a lifeguard must do is to identify the drowning victim. Being alert and aware of one's surroundings will help to identify someone who is drowning,

2) **Notification** – The lifeguard alerts help if needed. If no one else is around, the lifeguard will proceed to rescue the victim. If there are any bystanders, they usually begin to yell for help.

3) **Flotation** – The lifeguard brings a flotation device so that the victim will have something to hold on to until reaching the shore.

4) **Activation** – The lifeguard will act by jumping in the water and bringing the victim back to shore.

5) **Operation** – The lifeguard places his hands and arms under the victim in such a way that the water cannot pull the victim out of the lifeguard's arms. Likewise, when God rescues you, the devil cannot snatch you out of the arms of God! Have you ever been rescued by the Lord?

6) **Declaration** – While the lifeguard is pulling the victim back to safety, he is declaring to the victim that everything is going to be all right. The lifeguard is letting the victim know that although you were drowning, I am saving you and from this moment on everything is going to be all right.

7) **Observation** – Water can stay in your lungs for three to six hours after an incident. The lifeguard will not leave you after pulling you out to safety. When we pray for people who are drowning, it is crucial that we follow-up. Don't leave them because water might still be in their lungs. This is why some folk get saved on Sunday and they backslide on Tuesday. Water is still in their lungs. A real lifeguard will keep his eyes on the victim. God never leaves you. He is your lifeguard. He has brought you out of the water but some of the water is still in you. He may have brought you out of homosexuality, but it is still in you. He may have brought you out of your fornication, but every now and then you go back. He may have brought you out of gambling, but sometimes you still "scratch off" tickets. The lifeguard knows when there is still a little bit of

water in your lungs and it can suffocate you. God will never leave you and He will help to remove the remaining water from your lungs. He will help you receive total deliverance.

Why do people backslide? It is important to understand that no one just backslides. When people are drowning, God rescues them, but some people never sit down after God rescues them. Sitting down may be important, especially for those who still have water in their lungs. They are put back into serving too fast instead of being encouraged to take a break for restoration.

The lifeguard is still overseeing the pool. The people who were rescued and still have water in their lungs become agitated just sitting by the pool and begin to wave the lifeguard down. The lifeguard sees them, but pays no attention because they are not ready. They do not think there is any more water in their lungs, but the lifeguard knows how long they should sit down.

If you just went through a divorce, sit down, because you have water in your lungs! You lost your house and your car; sit down, you have water in your lungs! They just laid you off after twenty years and now you are bitter, sit down and hear from God; you have water in your lungs. If you have had any drowning in your life, you need to sit down and let God complete the process.

Don't make the mistake of leaving the area where the lifeguard is because you are being encouraged to sit for a while for restoration. Going to the pool down the street is not what you should do, because the lifeguard down the street does not know your DNA. He does not know what you need for complete healing and deliverance. So, if you jump into the water before you are ready, blood clots may start to form in your lungs. That will affect your mobile skills, which also affect your legs. You can begin to cramp and lose the ability to use your legs. You are drowning again; going through the same process over again, because you decided not to take the time to be restored. What if you had just sat down and obeyed the lifeguard assigned to your life ... the lifeguard who knows you?

The Power of Desperation

In Matthew 14, Peter was desperate to get closer to Jesus, even as He was walking on water. Peter asked the question in verse 28, "*Lord, if it be thou, bid me come unto thee on the water.*" In verse 29, Jesus answered Peter and said, "*Come.*" The power of desperation can cause a deaf man to hear, the power of desperation can cause the blind man to see, the power of desperation will cause the lame man to walk and even the dumb man to talk. The power of desperation can cause the rejected to succeed. Peter saw someone operating on a level that he desired. The anointing causes us to walk on what should have been over our heads but is now under our feet. He rescued Peter from sinking. He not only rescued Peter, but He also saved us from our drowning predicament! Give Him praise!

CHAPTER 4

GET YOUR FAITH WET

I believe God is saying, "I am not only your Savior, I am not only your deliverer, but I am also the one standing by you, walking beside you, and I am a very present help in the time of trouble. I want to get involved in your everyday life. I want to do some things for you that your eyes have not seen, neither have your ears heard. I want to move you in such a record number of ways that it will blow your mind. I want to do more for you than you have ever even imaged in your life. I am not a cosmic bully, waiting behind the bushes to kill, steal, and destroy you. No, I am a loving Father, I am a loving God, and I want to do something extra in your life. The only way that I am going to do something extraordinary in your life is if you invite me in."

That is what a lifeguard is all about. God is ready for you to tag Him in so He can get actively involved in your life. A lifeguard is a person who is responsible to ensure the safety of others from drowning. A lifeguard is often striving and sensing danger. The moment the lifeguard makes eye contact with the victim, he knows the victim is in need of being saved. Jesus Christ is the Lifeguard. In the realm of the spirit, a lifeguard is a person who carries an anointing that saves individuals from their drowning predicament.

I already ministered about sharks in the water, and you rescued me from drowning, but I want to stretch you a little bit and then stretch you some more. Not only does a lifeguard save you from drowning, but a real lifeguard will also teach you how to swim.

If you have financial difficulty or relational difficulty, if you suffered a divorce or sickness, if you are going through challenges in your marriage or on the job, God is here for you. If your bank account looks out of the ordinary, and it seems like the devil is trying to knock the wind out of your sails and cause you to drown in some type of predicament, God is here to save you. I am going to teach you to get back in the water! I know the enemy is trying to cause you to drown in some situations, but today you can get back in the water. I do not care what the enemy has said. I am ready to jump start you again and when I do, you will begin to swim like never before. It is time for you to swim again!

I know he cheated on you, but God said you are going to swim again. I know your house was foreclosed on, but that is not the only house God built. I know your car was repossessed, but that is not the only car that came out of the assembly line. You are going to swim again!

We know that a lifeguard not only saves people from drowning, but he also trains and develops swimmers. Get back in the water because God is going to give you strength. He is going to give you strength for your next swimming stroke. The enemy will try to bring fatigue and frustration, but you are closer to your destination—with your next stroke.

According to the National Institute of Mental Health, over 6.3 million people suffer from one or more diagnosed phobias. Although researchers have not determined exactly what causes a phobia, phobias are not a normal fear response. The definition of phobia is "a persistent act on the regular rational fear of a specific theme or situation that compels one to, in spite of the fact that he is not in danger." It is a persistent abnormal fear of a situation or thing that compels you to avoid it, knowing that the thing you are afraid of should not even hurt you.

2 Timothy 1:7 states, *"For God has not given us a spirit of fear but of power, love and a sound mind."* There are over one thousand recorded phobias: fear of needles, pointed objects, cats, getting a disease, pain, etc. Because you have the Holy Ghost inside you, and you are still settling for less when you know the best is on the inside, you evidently have a phobia that overcomes you. You are playing it safe, and you are not getting back in the water. God is getting ready to cause you to swim again!

Fear of colds, snow, money, etc. are actually more than fear, because the object of a phobia is not even dangerous. It exists only in your thinking. The devil is a liar! Go back and receive your promise. Go back to get every promise that God has ever spoken over your life. It doesn't matter how old you are. Believe God's Word and determine once and for all to believe that God has not given you a spirit of fear, but of love, power, and a sound mind.

Why? Because some of these phobias will keep you out of the water. If you've ever had a near-drowning experience, you have a phobia of getting back in the pool again. Even so, you know your creative genius comes out when you get in the right environment.

God gave me a vision of a fish that was still flipping on the beach. I picked up the fish and threw it back in the water. The lame and paralyzed looking fish that was on the seaside woke up when it got in its natural environment. The pool is a metaphor of your God-given natural environment of great potential. You will never come alive stuck on the side of the pool or the water's edge. You will come out alive when you get back in the water. Phobias of relational, situational, and sexual are because of fear. They will cause you to be stuck on the side and never get back into the water.

One of my favorite places to visit is Aruba. I've been there several times. In Aruba, we were on the beach. Life was good. My wife was looking good, and the beaches were beautiful. Someone said, "Travis, in the middle of the ocean, there is a fort almost the size of a football field and a half. We are getting ready to go there." Mind you, I have some swimming potential, so I know I can swim the full length. You can punk out in front of your girl if you like.

My wife said, "Go ahead and show them!" I taught all my children to swim, so I have the potential inside of me, too. She went on to say, "Take your time and whatever you do, keep breathing! Do not try to rush it. Stroke … breath, stroke … breath."

I dove into the water—stroke ... breath, stroke ... breath as she instructed. Yes, I made it there, and I prophesy that you are getting ready to do stroke and breath. You will get to the place called purpose and the place called destiny, because you are going to get your faith wet. It doesn't make any sense to drive ten or more hours to a gorgeous beach in Florida, purchase an expensive bathing suit and shades, and then never get into the water. You are too close to the pool to turn around now. Go ahead and dive in. Do not care what the devil says. The Word says in 1 John 4:4: *"Ye are of God, little children, and have overcome them: because greater is he that is in you, than he that is in the world."*

Every stroke needs a breath. Do not forget to breathe. Do not forget to inhale and exhale! Pace yourself and get back in the water. Are you tired of being stuck? John 5:1-9 states:

> *After this there was a feast of the Jews, and Jesus went up to Jerusalem.* [2] *Now there is in Jerusalem by the Sheep Gate a pool, which is called in Hebrew, Bethesda, having five porches. In these lay a great multitude of sick people, blind, lame, paralyzed, waiting for the moving of the water. For an angel went down at a certain time into the pool and stirred up the water; then whoever stepped in first, after the stirring of the water, was made well of whatever disease he had. Now a certain man was there who had an infirmity thirty-eight years. When Jesus saw him lying there, and knew that he already had been in that condition a long time, He said to him, "Do you*

want to be made well?" The impotent man answered Him, "Sir, I have no man to put me into the pool when the water is stirred up; but while I am coming, another steps down before me." Jesus said to him, "Rise, take up your bed and walk." And immediately the man was made well, took up his bed, and walked. And that day was the Sabbath"

How long will you be stuck by the pool, making excuses or concessions and wearing stylish sunglasses as you sip on a virgin pina colada? Will you be like a lot of people who drive ten plus hours to get to a beach and never get in the water? What is the water for? It is for stroking! When I first met you, you were a dreamer and could smell expectation. Now your greatest achievement is going to Kroger on double coupon day. I remember a time when you fervently and passionately took life and danced with it. Now you have taken off your dancing shoes and put them in the corner. You are just going through the motions. You are stuck. But God is getting ready to loose you from a place called stuck! God's Word says in Mark 10:46-47: "*And they came to Jericho: and as he went out of Jericho with his disciples and a great number of people, blind Bartimaeus, the son of Timaeus, sat by the highway side begging. And when he heard that it was Jesus of Nazareth, he began to cry out, and say, Jesus, thou son of David, have mercy on me.*"

When you get tired of always being a side dish, you will become the main course. Mark says the guy was at the pool, watching the stream of people go by. He was on the sidelines looking at everybody else in the stream of life. He

42

was begging, but the folks who were in the stream of life were not begging. My begging days are over! How about you? Let your begging days be over, too.

While people, who are on fire, are testifying, you are complaining that you were put out of your house and your car got repossessed. Your body is acting strangely, and jealousy and envy are setting in. Because you are not willing to make the faith commitment to walk your tests all the way out, you are going to short circuit and become jealous of the other man who was willing to make the faith commitment.

You cannot clock out on your faith! You have to make a faith commitment. You have to say, "Come hell or high water, I am going to sit here until my change comes! I am going to keep on confessing that Jesus was wounded for my transgressions. I am going to keep on confessing that He was bruised for my iniquity. The chastisement of my peace was laid on Him and with His stripes, I am healed. (see Isaiah 53:5) This must be your passionate resolve. Will you confess this? No one else can do this for you. It must be your determined testimony!

If you are not careful, the phobias will keep you on the sidelines. The Board of Health says that a phobia is a repeated exposure to the fear of their imagination. A phobia starts in the imagination. The Apostle Paul says in 2 Corinthians 10:4-5a, *"(For the weapons of our warfare are not carnal but are mighty through God to the pulling down of strongholds). Casting down every imagination ...."*

So the enemy sets up strongholds. That is why you want to check out and just settle for the side dish. You are not a side dish and you are not going to work a side hustle. You are not going to be stuck here. I know he left you with all the babies, but you are not going to be stuck here. Refuse to be in the same spot as you were two years ago. When depression comes, do not be there.

A phobia is a spirit that starts in your imagination. It starts in your head. Are you really going to make it? They are only voices in your head. Your fight is with the man in the mirror, telling you that you made a mistake—you failed. You are just like your mother. The devil does not play fair. He will break up your mother and your father. You have been in that same apartment since they built it, and that was twenty years ago. You say you are just afraid to get back in the stream of life again. You say you are, and they say you are not. You say you have been married for twenty years and you are just scared, so you put up with it. You say you are not sexually satisfied, spiritually satisfied, or financially satisfied.

These are phobias. He has been gone for three, four, or five years now, and you are still sleeping with his picture. Read Acts 26:2. Do you see yourself as happy King Agrippa? In this situation, fear and stress could have controlled Paul, but he took authority over them. King Agrippa is the enemy. He could have destroyed the Apostle Paul, but Paul said, "I think myself happy." You have authority over your happiness. You have to break the phobia. The fear of success, the fear of failure, the fear of prosperity, the fear of healing, and the fear of restoration—break it! You have to psych yourself out sometimes. Paul said, "I think myself happy. I am going to control my spirit in this hostile environment."

So we know that phobias start in the mind. The only way you can get free from a phobia is when you face it. I know you almost drowned last year, but now it is time to get back in the water again. Until you face it, you will never conquer it. You cannot conquer what you cannot confront. You have to confront this enemy and say according to Matthew 11:12: *"And from the days of John the Baptist until now the kingdom of heaven suffereth violence, and the violent take it by force."*

Yeah, I fell in some business situations. Yeah, I fell in some sexual relations, but I am in a new grace now. There is a new wind. There is a new anointing. There is a new shift in my life, and I believe this is my moment, this is my season, and this is God's time for me. You have to confront it. Call it out by its name.

James 2:18 says, *"Yea, a man may say, Thou hast faith, and I have works: shew me thy faith without thy works, and I will shew thee my faith by my works."*

Are you really in faith? If you haven't done anything, you are not in faith. If your faith is not in action, you are not in faith. Hebrews 11:6 says, *"But without faith it is impossible to please him: for he that cometh to God must believe that he is, and that he is a rewarder of them that diligently seek him."*

If I am not perfecting my craft, I am not in faith. If I'm not in faith, I'm not pleasing God. Romans 10:17 says,

"Faith cometh by hearing." I am going to challenge my fears and test the boundaries because there is more in me than meets the eye. I must have the right kind of faith in order to succeed and to swim in deep waters. Let's look at a few different types of faith:

> **Admirable Faith** – allows you to sit and admire the faith of others.

> **Academic Faith** – the kind of faith where you just study faith.

> **Argumentative Faith** – causes you to just argue the faith message.

> **Action Faith** – in order to try getting back into the water again, you need some action faith. I don't need admirable faith when I'm in a faith fight. I don't need academic faith when the devil is trying to kill me, and I do not need argumentative faith when the devil is trying to destroy my marriage. I need action faith! Why? Because I am putting my faith in action.

It is good to have admirable faith, academic faith, and argumentative faith, but you need action faith. You have deep water potential inside of you. Go ahead and jump in the water. He will save you. He will be there to the very end, and He will coach you to get to the other side.

CHAPTER 5

DIVE IN

Some of you are trying to swim and take off in the things of God, but you are in water that is too shallow. You cannot dive in shallow water. The reason you are getting tired and frustrated on this journey is because you are trying to dive in water that is too shallow.

Your conversations are shallow. Your seed sowing is shallow. The people you are hanging with are shallow. In this season of your life, you cannot try to get to this place called destiny and still be in shallow water. You can call me deep if you want. You can call me super spiritual, but I'm in a season of my life now where I do not have time for shallow people.

When someone is talking to me, and we do not even talk about the Lord Jesus Christ and what God is doing, something is wrong; and I need to check the connection. Christ should be the center of our conversations.

Whatever the case may be, I'm getting ready to leave this current place. I'm getting ready to press toward the mark of the higher prize and the call, which is in Christ Jesus. I'm pressing on.

The Dive Off

Now, I'm getting ready to take three large steps. Once divers take three steps, they are ready to dive in. I want you to understand how to dive off. If you watch any swimming star, such as Michael Phelps, you will notice they all have a great dive that gets them far out into the pool in very little time.

Last year, my daughter Destiny had her first swim meet. I remember it like it was yesterday. When the competitors were diving, they dived into the water and were almost to the other side. When they had the right form, they did not even have to come up to breathe. By the time they did come up, they were all ready to touch the wall and come back to the starting point. All of this was an indication that they knew how to breathe. "Just stroke and breathe."

I also remember when my daughter Destiny found out she would be diving into twelve feet. She said, "I cannot do that."

The lifeguard said, "Yes you can. When you dive, you are just going to come back up no matter how deep it is. You learned how to dive; if you can dive and you have the ability to come right back up, you can keep going no matter how deep it is.

I'm here to tell you that no matter how deep the water may seem, you can learn to dive in. You have to stop saying, "I've never done anything like this. I'm very fearful. I do not know how to do it. I do not know which way to go." God wants me to let you know that once you learn how to dive in, it doesn't matter how deep the water is. Once you learn how to dive, you can dive into twelve feet or any measure of water. Let me break this down for you.

Once you get your faith wet, once you start moving in the things of God, once you understand what faith really is, once you learn how to call those things that are not as though they were, once you understand that faith without works is dead, once you start walking on the water, once you start stepping out--you can dive in any depth of water.

Your Diving Position

The next thing I want to share with you about diving is your position. You have to be in a certain position when you dive. I think about it when my daughters are about to swim and also when I am reminiscing about growing up. When you grew up back in the old days, you knew that summer was all about swimming. If I could just get to the swimming pool and swim the whole day, I would be fine.

I can remember seeing others dive in and thinking, *I want to learn how to dive*. I could swim, but I could not dive. Isn't that something?

When they dived in, they went in headfirst. When most people jump into the water, they do not go in headfirst. They go in feet first. The reason you are not going anywhere is because you are going feet first instead of headfirst.

It is impossible to dive if you are trying to go feet first. How are you going to dive into the things of God? Isn't it amazing how you trust your feet more than you trust your head?

Clear the Ground before You Dive

My daughters are part of the swim team. If they have stuff in their way before they dive, then they're going to say, "I need you to move it out of the way." They make sure the people step back so they do not get hit. If you are getting ready to dive and you have people too close to you who are not ready to dive in, you have to clear the ground. You have to clear everything out.

The Bible says in Amos 3:3, "*Can two walk together, except they be agreed?*"

I'd like to see how there can be any movements if there is no agreement. The reason you are stopped smack in the middle of your dreams is because you are connected with people who don't have faith or they have little faith. The disciples asked Jesus to increase their faith. "*And the apostles said unto the Lord, Increase our faith. And the Lord said, If ye had faith as a grain of mustard seed, ye might say unto this sycamine tree, Be thou plucked up by the root, and be thou planted in the sea; and it should obey you*" (Luke 17:5-6).

You have to understand where people are around you. If they are not ready to dive in, if they are contemplating about the will of God concerning their lives, if they are worried about the next move, then they need to move out of your way because you are getting ready to dive in.

The Bible says: "Clear the grounds for the tents and make your tents large." We have to make room for the blessing of the Lord. It also says: "Spread out." You do know that you can have a large tent, but it may be too close to

50

someone else's tent—it is not spread out enough. Have you seen the kind of houses that are so close together it seems like you can reach out your window and touch somebody else's house? If something goes wrong in the house next door, I don't want it to affect my dwelling place. If the house next door catches fire, I do not have time for that fire to jump on me. Spread out!

Levels change and people do, too. I do not have a problem with your diving. I don't even have a problem with your living in your tent. All I'm saying is this, "Go all the way over there to set up your tent, because I know you. I can hear you saying, 'Can I borrow some of this? Can I have some of that?' No! I told you to go all the way over there."

The Bible says: "Spread out," and it also says: "Think big." God tells them to think big. Now, you would think that He would have said to think big before He said clear lots of ground. Instead, He wanted them to know that God is getting ready to move for you, but you are going to have to do something in order for God to move. We think that God is our dream genie. We think we're going to blink our eyes and it is going to happen—no, not in this season. You are going to have to get your help in Him and work your faith. *"Faith without works is dead."* (James 2:20) I call those things which be not as though they were (see Romans 4:17). You say, "Let there be this and that in the name of Jesus, and money cometh now." Well, you have to get up off the couch first. Work your faith.

God can take a barren woman who has never had a baby and cause her to end up with more children than most childbearing women. God wants you to clear lots of ground for your tents. Make your tents large, spread out, think big, use plenty of rope, and drive the "do not" pegs deep. You are going to need lots of elbowroom for your growing family. You are going to take over whole nations. You are going to resettle abandoned cities. Do not be afraid.

You are not going to be embarrassed. Do not hold back. You are not going to come up short—no, not this time. You will forget about all the humiliation of your youth. Tell yourself, "I will not hold back. I will not be ashamed this time." God needs you to clear lots of ground for your tents: make it large, spread out, think big, and drive the "do not" pegs in deep. Tell yourself, "I will not be shallow."

ABCs of Faith

Life has a way of causing one to check out in the middle of it. Have you ever been minding your own business, doing the will of God to your best ability, and all of a sudden, it seems as if all hell breaks loose? You did not ask for it, nor did you marry it, neither did you consider it. You did not see this in the forecast of your future, so instead of diving into the game of life, it causes you to just throw your hands up and say, "I quit. I quit serving in the church. I quit parenting. I quit this marriage. I give up on life." Life has a way of driving us to the place of saying things we really do not mean and will regret saying later.

It doesn't matter if God is telling you to start a company. It doesn't matter what God is telling you to do. When you learn the ABCs of having faith, you can dive into any water. A is for Ask. Ask and it shall be given. B is for

Believe. Believe and the door shall be opened. C is for Command. You have to command some things to come to pass according to the Word. D is for Demonstrate. You have to begin to demonstrate that which you believe. Tell yourself, "I have to learn the ABCs of faith."

CHAPTER 6

THE SHAMAR LIFEGUARD

In the Bible, God raised up Moses for the children of Israel. He raised up Joshua for his people. He even raised up Esther for the Jews. Man was in sin so far from God that He raised up a lifeguard by the name of Jesus. Jesus Christ is our Lifeguard. God raises up lifeguards anytime the people of God are in a drowning predicament. A lifeguard is a person who carries an anointing to get you out of your drowning situation and to move you into a state of winning in life.

Psalms 127:1 says: *"Except the Lord builds the house, they labour in vain that build it: except the Lord keep the city, the watchman waketh but in vain."* The key word in this Scripture is "keep." The word "keep" means *shamar*. I want to deal with the *shamar* lifeguard. We are going to receive revelation, implementation, preservation, and activation. We are going to get a revelation of the *shamar* lifeguard. Then we are going to begin to implement that revelation. Through implementation, God will bring preservation. Finally, we will be able to walk in full activation.

Shamar means to guard, to keep, and to be a watchman. It can refer to guarding a flock, the heart, the mind, a nation, or a city from outside attack or ungodly influences. It is used in reference to keeping (guarding) the gates or entries to cities. Each local church needs a prophetic guard. This is not one prophet, but a company of prophets who help guard the church from the invasion of the enemy.

Churches that develop the prophetic ministry will have the advantage of being protected through prophetic intercession and the *shamar* aspect of the prophetic ministry.

To guard means a number of things. It can mean to protect, to watch over, to stand guard over, to police, to secure, to defend, to shield, to shelter, to screen, to cover, to cloak, to preserve, to save, to conserve, to supervise, to keep under surveillance or control, to keep under guard, to govern, to restrain, to suppress, to keep watch, to be alert, or to take care.

Synonyms for guard include: protector, defender, guardian, custodian, watchman, sentinel, sentry, patrol, and garrison. These words help us visualize and define the *shamar* aspect of the prophetic ministry.

The Church has often assumed that pastors are spiritual guardians of the Church while neglecting to see the role and the ministry of prophets. The Church, however, was never intended to function with only pastors serving as protectors of the people.

1 Corinthians 12:28 says: "*And God hath set some in the church, first apostles, secondarily prophets, thirdly*

teachers, after that miracles, then gifts of healings, helps, governments, diversities of tongues." So now we see the foundation of the Church.

The foundation of the Church is not pastors. The foundation of the Church is apostles and then prophets. Churches cannot ignore the ministry of the prophet. Prophets have also been set in the Church to help fulfill the important role of protecting the house.

I want you to think about the church that you are currently connected to or even the one you came out of. It is not a bad church. God is pleased with them. Miracles, healing, and salvation happen there. But is there a strong prophetic culture at that particular place?

If you are not careful, you will think that God only uses what is familiar, what our brains can comprehend.

God lets us know that if His house is going to be what He designed it to be, then the ministry of the prophet has to come forth.

Ministry of the Prophet

Let's look at Hosea 12:13 that says: "*And by a prophet the Lord brought Israel out of Egypt, and by a prophet was he preserved.*" God was reveals to us that one of the major functions of the prophet's ministry is preservation. Israel was delivered from Egypt through the ministry of the Prophet Moses. Then Israel was preserved through the intercession of the Prophet Moses. In Numbers 14:11-20, God was getting ready to destroy Israel. It took a prophet to intercede for the people. God preserved them because of the prophetic ministry of Moses.

The word "preserve" means to keep, keep from harm, keep from damage, keep from danger, and keep from evil. It also means to protect and to serve. The Hebrew translation of the word "preserve" means *shamar,* which means to hedge about, to guard, to protect, to watch, and to keep.

The word *shamar* is first used in Genesis 2:15, which says: *"And the Lord God took the man, and put him into the Garden of Eden to dress it and to keep it."* The word "keep" in the Hebrew language means to *shamar.* Adam was expected to guard the garden, to preserve it, and to hedge about it. Why would God give man the commandment and the responsibility to *shamar,* to keep, to guard, and to protect something that was not worth anything? God knew that His greatest investment was in His church. His greatest investment was in the people of God. Since we cannot protect ourselves, God sends a *shamar* prophet to guard His investment that He has placed inside of you.

That is good news! Nothing will be lost! God is going to take the scraps of your life and weave them together and produce the greatest manuscript known to man. How? God will send a *shamar* lifeguard to protect and hedge around his investment.

The *shamar* anointing is coming back to the kingdom! The word *shamar* emphasizes the protective element of the prophet's mantle. The preserving and guarding aspect of this prophetic anointing is needed in every house and in every local church. What about churches that do not embrace the prophetic house of the prophetic anointing? What if you have houses that do not have the *shamar* anointing—a *shamar* lifeguard who is protecting what comes in and what goes out?

Can I tell you what is going to be in those houses? The absence of a shamar anointing and shamar lifeguard opens the atmosphere to perversion. When you are under a *shamar* anointing, the prophet is able to stand up in the pulpit and say, "Other people may do that, but not you because of where you are going." We all need someone to watch over us. We need somebody who can see a little further in the realm of the spirit than we can. Thank God for the prophetic ministry.

The prophetic ministry is more than, "I see a house, I see a car." The prophetic ministry is more than, "In three days, you are going to get this." The prophetic ministry looks into the future and says, "I see the enemy coming to the camp. Make sure all of the gates are closed. Close the gates!" That is what a watchman does. A watchman will stand on his post and will see what the enemy is trying to do and counteracts his plan. That is why cancer cannot come into our houses. When there is a *shamar* lifeguard prophetic anointing on guard, the house is protected from disease. Even the death angel will have to pass over a protected house. Stand guard!

Guard the Gates

Something is wrong in the house of God. We have too much coming in that God never ordained. We have to guard the gates. We need intercessors who will guard the gates. We are not supposed to be poor. However, a spirit of poverty and spirit of lack have come into the Church. Somebody has not been guarding the gates. You are blessed. Don't be satisfied with poverty. Stand on your watch and say, "Devil, in the name of Jesus, you will not come in! Loose that man. Loose that boy. I command the riches of heaven to come upon the people of God in Jesus' name." You want your sister to be blessed? You want your brother to be wealthy? You want those around you to be blessed? Of course you do. So guard the gates.

Guard the gates!

You know something has happened to the guarding of the gates when you see men acting like women and women acting like men. Homosexuality is in a lot of churches. We have to guard the gates. Divorce is in all churches. We have to guard the gates. A spirit of Jezebel has come in the Church when you cannot find a submitted wife or a submitted husband. Wives are not submitting to their husbands. Husbands are not submitting to God. What has happened? A spirit has come in unaware. The reason many singles do not want to get married is because of the example they see in the Church. There are very few good examples of Godly marriages in the house of God. We must do a better job of guarding the gates.

Jude 1:3 says: *"Beloved, when I gave all diligence to write unto you of the common salvation, it was needful for me to write unto you, and exhort [you] that ye should earnestly contend for the faith which was once delivered unto the saints."* Jude was the half-brother of Jesus. He writes this letter and says: "contend," which means fight or engage in war. Sometimes, you have to fight to keep God's agenda. It is a spirit that causes a woman to leave her husband. It is a spirit that causes a man to leave his wife and all of his children. That is not natural for God's people. Not even dogs and lions do that. Bears do not do that. A spirit has crept in because somebody was not on his post. Somebody was not guarding the gates.

Spirit of Religion

Jude 1:4 says: "*For there are certain men crept in unawares, who were before of old ordained to this condemnation, ungodly men, turning the grace of our God into lasciviousness, and denying the only Lord God, and our Lord Jesus Christ.*" Somebody was sleeping, and it crept in. The local church is kept safe through the prophetic intercession, the prophetic discernment, prophetic praise, prophetic teaching, prophetic preaching, and prophetic worship. What does all of that mean? A spirit of religion is from the enemy and religion keeps us stagnated—in the same place and never abounding in growing. Furthermore, it means that you are in a church that goes through the same rituals every Sunday.

You can almost clock what is going to happen next. "She is going to dance here. He is going to get up and say, 'Yes, Lord' there." You can even clock when the preacher is ready to turn it up. When you can clock stuff, it loses its spontaneity, and it goes into a religious order or a very stiff traditional order.

Jesus said the reason I could not move like I wanted to move is because your tradition hindered me. Your tradition hindered my power. Your tradition hindered my miracles. What you need is prophetic worship to take the place of pathetic worship. What is prophetic worship? It is worship that causes you to say, "I know we have four songs to go, but there is a word in that one song that is really bringing healing and deliverance to the people. We need to stay right there and let God finish doing what God started in the first place."

Sometimes, we do not need to move to what is next. Sometimes, we do not need to move to the next agenda if God is healing—if God is breaking the fallow ground . . . if God is mending people back together. Let God have His way. Sometimes, the Holy Spirit can download a song that bubbles up in your spirit. The worship leader cannot be hindered by the pressure of going to the next song.

When the worship leaders first came to our ministry, they were stuck in tradition. They knew nothing about the song of the Lord. I told them to learn how to recognize the move of God so they would know when to pause, stay right there, and hear what God was saying. After you sit in the presence of God long enough, you learn to stop allowing yourself to be rushed.

Psalms 68:8 says: *"The earth shook, the heavens also dropped at the presence of God: even Sinai itself was moved at the presence of God, the God of Israel."* The Hebrew word for dropped is *nataph*, which means to drop, drip, ooze, preach, or prophesy. *Nataph* happens during worship as the

Lord "drops" a song from heaven as a result of His presence. It is like the dew in the morning. It builds up. Sometimes, you cannot rush the presence of God. What does this have to do with the *shamar*?

Have you ever been in a service and you know the presence of God has changed the speaker's message and you have gotten a direct word from God that hits your heart, touches your spirit, and changes your life? What if somebody was trying to keep up with an agenda? That preacher or that person would be accountable. You are messing with people's lives. Stop rushing. They need all of God.

You say, "Let me say this and then I will get out of your way?" No! Stay there long enough to create an atmosphere. We are tired of the flesh. We need people who can create an atmosphere where signs, wonders, and miracles can take place. Every song should not be sung. Just because it is gospel does not mean it is anointed. Shut the gates! Watch the gates!

Create an Atmosphere

Everything cannot go on in the house of God. I thank God for gospel rap, but we have to be careful when gospel rap turns into hip-hop rap. I have no problem when the girls are dancing and we are praising God, but we have to be careful when the girls start twerking and start doing splits and dropping it like it is hot. What does that have to do with the anointing of God?

Furthermore, you need to check who you have leading the worship. You cannot wear the same clothes you once wore to the club. You should not want to wear anything that will seduce anyone. No, it is not sin. It is not unlawful, but it is not expedient.

There is so much going on now with God's people. Married couples are swapping mates. Yes, swinging is in the Church. Know that in God's house, there is only one couple in the bedroom—one couple who is in covenant with God in marriage. Who is going to be the guard against lasciviousness and perversion? Who is going to be the one who keeps watch? Who is going to be the watchman?

Something has come in so much so that the fear of God is no longer in the Church. You are a woman of God and your cleavage is showing? We wear all types of damnable things that have been offered up to idols. You need to stop wearing symbols of which you do not know the meaning. Something has come up in the Church. God sends a *shamar* prophet, a *shamar* lifeguard to warn the body. Though the world is doing it, it shouldn't be named among us. The local church needs a prophetic guard.

Leaders cannot sleep around with the women in the church. What happened to accountability? If you mess up, you need to sit down and repent openly. You cannot preach and sin at the same time. The people will get a false revelation that they can do the same thing. Go for deliverance. Stop sleeping with your sons and daughters. That is why the *shamar* lifeguard comes in—to guard, to protect, to defend, and to carry the Church.

The Bible says: *"Except the Lord build the house, they labour in vain that build it: except the Lord keep the city, the watchman waketh but in vain"* (Psalm 127:1). Except the Lord *"shamar"* the city, guard the city, then the things that are not of God can come into the city. Father, watch over cities, our churches, and our homes.

Some people say they have feelings toward the same sex and they are tired of hindering who they are. We all have feelings, but we do not ride on our feelings; instead, we nail our feelings to the cross. Furthermore, we cannot walk in lawlessness. This means that you live a life without any rules and you think you can do whatever you want to do. The Bible says, *"Know ye that the Lord he is God: it is he that hath made us, and not we ourselves; we are his people, and the sheep of his pasture"* (Psalm 100:3). You've been bought with a price. You do not belong to yourself.

The reason I come against homosexuality is because it is a ruling principality in many major cities. I am not coming against the person. If you are a homosexual or if you are a lesbian, I love you with the love of Jesus. I love you and hate the sin. However, I am not going to shut my mouth against the devil. *"For this purpose the Son of God was manifested, that he might destroy the works of the devil"* (1 John 3:8b).

Homosexuality exists, even in the Church, from the leadership down. The Bible tells us in Leviticus 18:22 that *"thou shalt not lie with mankind, as with womankind: it is abomination."* It is a spirit that needs to be cast out of the Church. I did not say cast the people out, I said cast the spirit

65

out. It takes the ministry of the prophetic *shamar* lifeguard to identify, confront, and cast out the spirits that are not of God. Why? Because if that spirit stays at your church or stays at your house, it is possible that it will affect you. You cannot fry fish and not come out with that aroma.

Guard the gates. Guard the gates!

The prophetic lifeguards who have been assigned to the Church have a spirit of discernment to identify, confront, and cast out spirits that are not of God before they become mature spirits. Be a lifeguard in your house for your children. Do not be too busy to watch and pray over them—to recognize when the enemy is trying to come in. Understanding the power of generational curses, you particularly need to pray that the strongholds you have been delivered from don't try to attach themselves to your children. James 5:16 says: "*The effectual fervent prayer of a righteous man availeth much.*" Be the *shamar* lifeguard who guards the gates praying, "In the name of Jesus, I plead the blood. I command that spirit to lose my son, to lose my daughter.

Are you guarding or are you enabling? It is not a good thing to enable people who are intentionally walking in sin. It is enabling when you are keeping the children of a mother who goes out every night and continues to get pregnant after having unprotected sex with different men. It is enabling when you continue to give money to family members who suffer from drug addiction. If you keep playing with the enemy, he is going to destroy you. We have to love the person and hate the sin.

Psalms 130:6 says: "*My soul waiteth for the Lord more than they that watch for the morning: I say, more than they that watch for the morning.*"

In Isaiah 62:6, the Bible says: "*I have set watchmen upon thy walls, O Jerusalem, which shall never hold their peace day nor night: ye that make mention of the Lord, keep not silence.*" What am I doing right now? I am not holding my peace. I know you may not like this, but someone has to stand on the watch. Someone has to cry out loud and spare not.

There is a marriage-breaking spirit that is loose in the land. A spirit of adultery is loose in the land. Are you a married man and the enemy has you looking at pornography? Are you going to the strip club? The Bible says, "*Neither give place to the devil*" (Ephesians 4:27).

What does light and darkness have in common? Nothing! So why are you getting advice from worldly women about your godly marriage? Bad communication corrupts good manners. If I am connected to someone who is evil, they will eventually poison me. If we are not careful, those evil spirits that we allow to come in will destroy us and will destroy the anointing of the house. We then have a whole bunch of sexually perverted people in the church.

Some say it is alright just to have oral sex when you are not married, but the Bible says: "*Know ye not that your body is the temple of the Holy Ghost which is in you, which ye have of God, and ye are not your own? For ye are bought with a price: therefore glorify God in your body, and in your spirit, which are God*" (1 Corinthians 6:19-20). If you defile your temple, God said he will destroy you. *"If any man defile the temple of God, him shall God destroy; for the temple of God is holy, which temple ye are"* (1 Corinthians 3:17).

Some people have gone through some devastating times in their lives because of rape, molestation, etc. God is able to heal your hurt and bring deliverance and healing into your life. Do not allow the enemy to tell you that you have to be a certain way because of what happened to you. In other words, he wants to justify your sinning. No! Be who God has called you to be. Walk in victory and not in sin. Tell the devil he is a liar and curse him back to the pits of hell.

Just because wearing tattoos is popular, and people who you hold in high esteem wear them, doesn't make it right. The Bible tells us that it is an abomination. *"Ye shall not make any cuttings in your flesh for the dead, nor print any marks upon you: I am the Lord"* (Leviticus 19:28). I do not care who has a tattoo, it is not right. The Church is so busy trying to act like the world, yet the world is busy trying to act like the Church.

You have to come out from among them. *"Wherefore come out from among them, and be ye separate, saith the Lord, and touch not the unclean thing; and I will receive you"* (2 Corinthians 6:17). If you know the Scriptures, why not obey them?

The enemy will have you on a sugar crave and make you think you need to keep a certain high. You feel like you are nothing without that high. He will have you saying, "I'm just lonely. I need the company of the opposite sex." The enemy has you in depression, and anytime you get lonely, the devil comes into a door. Anytime you get stressed, anytime you get very antsy, your ungodly fulfillment of the void that you have becomes your drug of choice. Whatever your drug of choice is, it is going to kill you if you don't bind up the enemy.

The Bible says we are all drawn away with our own lusts and enticed, but when it is over, it is going to defeat you. (see James 1:14). We are building a hedge of protection, and the prophetic spiritual authority acts as the fence or garrison around an assigned congregation. God sends prophetic lifeguards and assigns them to a congregation so the congregation will not be affected by the enemy. God put our church in this particular territory for a reason. The reason was holiness. The reason was to be a light in darkness and let the city know there is a group of people who are crying loudly and sparing not in telling you that you can live holy in an unholy world. You can live free because *"if the Son therefore shall make you free, ye shall be free indeed"* (John 8:36). God is able to keep you from falling. *"He is able to keep you from falling and present you faultless"* (Jude 1:24). You do not have to fall again.

You are in trouble if you are sitting in a church that tells you, "Every now and then, you can fall on something. Nobody is perfect. Nobody is right. Everybody sins." The devil in hell is a liar. The Bible says, *"Follow peace with all men, and holiness, without which no man shall see the Lord"* (Hebrews 12:14). Holiness is the answer for the world, and you cannot be holy without the Holy Ghost. A long time ago, you could minister this type of word and the whole church would say, "Yes, Lord." Something has come in that makes it hard for the people to say "Amen."

The Bible says, *"And I will give you pastors according to mine heart, which shall feed you with knowledge and understanding"* (Jeremiah 3:15). God said He gave pastors according to His heart and not ours. Our hearts can be wicked. Jeremiah says: *"The heart is deceitful above all things, and desperately wicked: who can know it"* (Jeremiah 17:9).

"Wisdom is the principal thing; therefore get wisdom: and with all thy getting get understanding" (Proverbs 4:7). Do you see how the enemy is trying to desensitize us? When you see two men kissing nowadays, it is nothing. A long time ago, if you saw two men in the same bed, you said, "Turn off the TV." When you see two women kissing, to some people, it is a turn on. The Bible says in Romans 1:18-21:

> *For the wrath of God is revealed from heaven against all ungodliness and unrighteousness of men, who hold the truth in unrighteousness; Because that which may be known of God is manifest in them; for God hath shewed it unto them. For the invisible things of him from the creation of the world are clearly seen, being understood by the things that are made, even his eternal power and Godhead; so that they are without excuse: Because that, when they knew God, they glorified him not as God, neither were thankful; but became vain in their*

imaginations, and their foolish heart was darkened.

What does wrath mean? It means judgment, the anger of God. God is angry when we break a covenant. How do you hold the truth? For instance, when you are still fornicating and committing adultery, but you know it is wrong. You are holding the truth in unrighteousness. You know you have diabetes, and you are still eating cake. You know better, but you will not do better.

Look at verses 22-24 of Romans 1: *"Professing themselves to be wise, they became fools, And changed the glory of the uncorruptible God into an image made like to corruptible man, and to birds, and fourfooted beasts, and creeping things. Wherefore God also gave them up to uncleanness through the lusts of their own hearts, to dishonour their own bodies between themselves."*

If you keep playing with ungodliness, God is going to give you over to it. If you keep praying against the moving of God, keep being rebellious, there will be consequences. There is going to come a time when you are praying for repentance and God will say, "I am not going to hear you because I gave you over to that."

Sometimes, we think the only sins are sexual sins, but what about rejection, bitterness, and offense? The spirit of offense is so heavy in the body of Christ now. And you think just because you are angry and offended, it gives you a right to sin. No, the Bible says: *"Work out your own salvation with fear and trembling"* (Philippians 2:12b). So you cannot go to God and say, "Father, I went to a church

71

and a certain person sinned, too." No! The Bible says in 18:12: "*So then every one of us shall give account of himself to God.*" What is God going to say?

Can you see why the worship is so heavy in churches around America? Do you notice how we have to press in to worship? It is because of all the demon spirits that are prevalent in the Church. People are not coming to get free; they are coming for religious entertainment. The Bible says, "*Wherefore God also gave them up to uncleanness through the lusts of their own hearts, to dishonour their own bodies between themselves:*" (Romans 1:24).

Lawlessness

Some people are living life in lawlessness. They feel as though they don't have to listen to anyone. The Bible also says: "*Submit yourselves to every ordinance of man for the Lord's sake: whether it be to the king, as supreme; Or unto governors, as unto them that are sent by him for the punishment of evildoers, and for the praise of them that do well*" (1 Peter 2:13-14).

Back in the day, if a man of God said something, we listened to him. Now, let a man of God tell you something that you, in your flesh, do not want to hear, you will not obey what has been said. Why? Because the spirit of lawlessness is in the land. It says, "I do not care what you say. I am going to do it my way." That same person will go to prayer and talk to the Father. That is scary. You can be disobedient with the man of God, but you will talk to God the Father. Do you not understand that the Father gave you the man of God? You may not be a homosexual, a fornicator, or an adulterer, but

72

there is a spirit of lawlessness somewhere when you say, "We are not going to follow the Word all the way." The Bible says: *"There is a way that seemeth right unto a man, but the end thereof are the ways of death"* (Proverbs 16:25).

I've told people, "I think this guy is gay; leave him alone." They spit in my face and did not believe me. I have told others, "I do not think that job is for you. You are barely saved and you will not have any time in the kingdom." I did not volunteer the advice; they came to me seeking wisdom. I don't understand why some people would even have a *shamar* lifeguard, because they listen to everybody else saying, "Oh, Travis doesn't know what he is talking about." Go back to them if you want to and walk away from the wisdom that God has given me to share.

God would never give you a prophet for you to close your eyes on. You may not understand it, and you may not like it. Swallow your spit and keep on worshipping, because I guarantee you, you may not see it today, but give it some time, and the wisdom that has been spoken will prove to be true.

Many of us are more concerned about our outer appearance than we are with who we are on the inside. What if we had *shamar* lifeguards in every local church who would teach men and women how to be holy?

Some people think you cannot wear makeup and be holy. I have no problem with makeup; for some it is a cosmetic blessing. However, do not allow your physical appearance to mean more to you than exemplifying who God wants you to be according to His Word.

It is amazing how people dress up on the outside, but they are not right on the inside. We make so many excuses for our sin. If we cover our sins, we will not prosper. (see Proverbs 28:13)

God's Original Plan

We have covered areas that show how we have drifted away from God's original plan. Adam was given the Garden of Eden to *shamar* it, keep it, and to guard it. How did the serpent get in? Some people say the serpent was always there. I do not believe that. My great aunts were farmers and I remember going to Helen, Georgia and South Georgia. They would till the ground. The ground did not have any type of snakes and predators when they were doing the tilling. When the vegetation started coming up, it attracted outside predators. What if Adam had killed the serpent because it was attracted to the fruit? The devil is attracted to your fruit, attracted to your anointing. It takes a *shamar* anointing to cut the head off the serpent before it destroys the fruit. You have fruit inside of you and the devil is after it.

We can no longer sit in our churches and be "dumbed down" anymore. We can no longer sit in our churches and only hear about "Mary had a little lamb." The lamb was also the Lion of Judah who came and shed His blood on the cross, so that we may have everlasting life when we receive Him—the lamb who also has all power in His hand to provide us with the authority we need to break the back of the enemy and put our families back together. Adam had a responsibility to *shamar* the garden, to keep the garden. It was his responsibility and not Eve's.

The Bible says: "*Husbands, love your wives, even as Christ also loved the church, and gave himself for it*" (Ephesians 5:25). Christ never beat the Church, never choked the Church, never raped the Church, and never gave the Church a black eye. He gave His life for His bride. We need more men who will give their lives for their wives. I'm tired of hearing men say, "She's crazy." In actuality, you are "punking out" when you resort to blaming the other person.

Even when His bride spat in his face, Christ still died for her. What if we had men to love their families like Christ loves the Church? What if we had men to come back to the house? He might be there, but he is not completely there. Something else is taking his attention away from his own house.

While David was helping another man's battle, his house was left unguarded. The devil came in and stole his wife and burned up his house. (see 1 Samuel 30:1-3) Anytime you start worrying about trying to help somebody else's house and leave your own house unguarded, the enemy is going to come in and try to destroy your family. God, bring the man back to his family. I call his mind back. I call his attention back. I call his affections back to his house.

When the man is not there, physically or mentally, his wife can feel it. She can see him wandering off. Everyone else is watching television, being a family, and he is somewhere else. He calls it working or he says he needs some down time. His attention is somewhere else, and whoever has his attention has his heart.

The enemy comes in just like that. Our young people see their mom and dad so separate, and now they are full of rebellion because they are full of rejection. Rejection has to cling onto rebellion. You may have been rejected because of your size, your weight, your color, your height, or your hair. Anyone with any type of difference has to go for deliverance from rejection. Someone or something rejects you, and then you grow up saying, "I do not need them. I do not care." Rejection has to connect to rebellion, and rebellion is situated with pride. Pride is going to justify your rebellion. You say, "The reason I am like that is because they did this and they did that. Or the reason I am like this is because God made me this way." The devil in hell is a liar. God did not make you that way. He made you holy and you have messed up His plan by walking in rebellion. The Bible says we were *"created in Christ Jesus unto good works, which God hath before ordained that we should walk in them"* (Ephesians 2:10).

Issues of Dating

What is wrong with dating? Every time you date, you have an increased chance of fornicating – that is what's wrong with dating. Some of you have found out that every time you dated, you fornicated; you fell. Dating doesn't work for you. How many times are you going to fall before you change your heart and your actions? I am not talking about people who are not saved. I am talking about people who are saved and know what the Word says, but refuse to do the Word and continue to walk in sin.

Allow the Lifeguard to rescue you from your drowning predicament. He is here to help you. Call for help.

Cover Your Marriage

I have nothing against pursuing marriage. I believe you are supposed to be married. Now, if you are married to a crack addict who is not the person God prepared for you, that is on you. I believe you are supposed to be married to a person who loves God. Everybody who is engaged to someone whom you believe is your potential person, you have to realize that you have to have more than his name; you need to have his nature. Everybody who is saved has the name of Jesus, but do they have His nature? Are you loving, kind, long suffering, gentle, meek, good, and have faith? Being married to a woman can be long suffering.

If a man doesn't have the nature of Jesus, when he gets into a toxic season, whatever is already in him is going to come up. You are going to be surprised when it manifests. The first thing you are going to say is, "I thought you were saved; I thought you loved the Lord." If the man you are with does not have the nature of Jesus, he is liable to curse out you and your God.

All of this stuff is coming into the Church and invading our lives. We need prophetic *shamar* lifeguards to say, "No! I am closing the door. I cannot look at certain shows on television. I do not look at certain movies from certain genres of people because they are full of lust. I do not look at horror movies because they are full of death.

Many of the demons that we are fighting in our houses come in through the television or other media. If you know the enemy uses the Internet to lure you into chat rooms or places you shouldn't be entertaining. You need an accountability person if you truly want to be free. You know you cannot handle it by yourself. You do not need to be in an apartment by yourself.

You have to know where you are in this season. You need someone to *shamar* you—someone to cover you. You hesitate about being transparent because you do not want anyone to think you are not saved. I did not say you were not saved. I did not say you were not anointed. I just said you were fighting some things. What if our forefathers would have seen this? There are many times when even wayward renegades join the Church and sow seeds of discord. If you are not watchful, you will not know to go into warfare when you see a spirit coming.

The Spirit of Jezebel Separates

What hates the prophetic house? Jezebel. Jezebel hates the prophetic spirit. She can say something sweet about the prophet, but her heart hates it. Understand, she doesn't hate the person. She hates the office of the prophet. When you do research on the name Jezebel, you will find that it means prince. Now, why would she be a prince when she should be a princess? She is out of order.

Moreover, in a prophetic house, Jezebel hates prophets. Jezebel does not target women only. There are a lot of men with Jezebel spirits—very controlling, very manipulative, and very schizophrenic. Have you ever seen a schizophrenic pastor? One Sunday, he is word of faith, and another Sunday, he is Pentecostal. Every time a new doctrine comes in, he teaches it. Who are we? The name of the church changes at least five times a year. The vision always changes. First you are after the lost, and now you are after the found.

I believe change is good and God can bring evolution to the vision, but when you are in a prophetic, apostolic house, you have to understand that Jezebel is a spirit, and it will attach itself to a man or woman. The first thing Jezebel does is separate herself from the people. Why? Because she is getting ready to form her own church. People who always rebel against the leader of the church circle themselves with Jezebel. They normally start like this. "How was church? It was all right. I am so sick of church. I am so churched out." You are sitting there saying, "But you have church every Sunday; you are the first one to give an offering." The Bible says there are seven things God hates. One is a person who sows discord among the brethren. The Bible never says God hates a fornicator, but it does say he hates a gossiper (see Proverbs 6:16-19).

Jezebel brings a spirit of discord to try to divide the church. Even though the worship is high, Jezebel will sit in church like there is no mighty moving of God. It will attach itself to a prophetic house, and the only way to dethrone Jezebel is to call it out. The Jezebel spirit is controlling and manipulative. No one else can say anything because that spirit has made up its mind that it is right.

If you work all the time, you cannot listen to anything. If you are full of bitterness, if you have been rejected, and if you have been abused, you should come to church and sit down and get healed. But Jezebel cannot sit down. Why? She has to lead. Have you ever seen an Ahab husband and a Jezebel wife? A man with an Ahab spirit allows his wife to speak in every situation; he rarely says anything (see 1 Kings Chapters 18-20).

In this situation, you have a man who thinks he is highly anointed and has to always speak. The Jezebel spirit sucks the prophetic out of the church. The people of God cannot sit in church and pray that they don't get another prophecy. If you do not get another prophecy, you are not going to make it; because God said the foundation of the Church is the prophets.

Some may think that many of the people on television, who profess to be prophets, are nothing more than pulpit pimps and that all prophets are that way. No! God has ordained the true prophets. You do have pulpit pimps but that does not mean there are no true prophets. God does nothing in the earth except He gives it to His prophets (see Amos 3:7). If Jezebel controls the house, it sucks the prophetic out of the house. If a house is so divided, faith cannot come alive. What causes the prophetic to be at its all-time high? Faith. When the faith goes up, the windows open up and you can see. But when division is in the church, discord is in the church.

Jezebel cannot be a silent member of the church; she has to be in leadership of the church. Your leader may say, "Everyone, we are wearing green." Jezebel will secretly say, "Put on black," because she cannot submit. That is one word that we never heard taught, because the person who has to teach has to submit himself.

Activating the Shamar

The prophet's anointing carries with it the ability to activate. Prophets have the ability through prophesying not only to impart but also to stir up and ignite ministries and gifts within individuals. The breath of God is released through prophesying, and life is imparted and activated.

The prophet Ezekiel was commanded by the Lord to prophesy to the dry bones: So I prophesied as he commanded me, and the breath came into them, and they lived, and stood upon their feet, and exceeding great army. (Ezekiel 37:10).

With prophetic activation, local assemblies will have greater strength and proper form. People will come into their position. When people are out of position in the local assembly, the result is confusion. The prophetic ministry can also activate miracles, healings, signs, and wonders within the local assembly. All of the gifts if the Spirit are activated through prophetic ministry.

When the enemy tries to present some very damnable gospels and heresies, the *shamar* lifeguard must be on duty to cast him out of our houses and out of our churches. As we receive the blessings and the abundance that God has for us, He has to remain our focus. We cannot get to the point where we allow the things of this world to become our point of worship. Romans 1:25 says: *"Who changed the truth of God into a lie, and worshipped and served the creature more than the Creator, who is blessed forever."* Everything belongs to Him. Keep it, guard it—*shamar* it.

Our worship should be pointed to God—the One who made heaven and earth. The One who comes to our rescue and keeps us from drowning. He is our Lifeguard. Help is on the way!

ABOUT THE AUTHOR

Travis C. Jennings, founder and Senior Pastor of The Harvest Tabernacle Church in Atlanta, Georgia, is a celebrated speaker and author. Apostle Jennings' revelatory, bold, and cutting-edge delivery makes him one of the most prominent, unique and authentic leaders today.

He is a passionate prophetic life coach, creative visionary, successful entrepreneur, gospel producer, and philanthropist. His weekly television broadcast, *End-Time Harvest with Travis and Stephanie Jennings*, airs weekly on WATC-TV and reaches millions of homes with the life-changing ministry of Jesus Christ.

Contact Information:

Harvest Tabernacle Church
1450 South Deshon Road
Lithonia, GA 30058
tsjbookings@gmail.com
www.theharvesttabernacle.org

CPSIA information can be obtained at www.ICGtesting.com
Printed in the USA
LVOW08s0542251114

415416LV00004B/5/P

9 780692 299173